DREAMS

WELBECK
CHILDREN'S BOOKS

First published in the US in 2025
by Welbeck Children's Books
An imprint of Hachette Children's Group

The publishers would like to thank the following sources for their kind permission to reproduce the pictures in this book.

GETTY IMAGES: Ksenia Butakov cover, 1C, 3C. SHUTTERSTOCK: All images GoodStudio apart from: alyonaz 65BR; bartama_graphic 19TR; BRO.vector 45C; Charlottstudio 41BR; delcarmat 7B, 56BL, 57BL; Edge Creative 64R; Eksall 4TR, 68CR, 69BR; FFFLOW 66BR; Iconic Prototype 40R; Inamiqu 40C; inspiring.team 33TR; IrinaShcherbakova 45BR; ivector 53BL; klyaksun 59TR; lemono 9BL, 38BC, 41L; Macrovector 58CR; mentalmind 8BL, 8BC, 12CR, 13TL, 41C, 61BR; Merfin 10TR; Lova Mikhailova 63CR; Evgeniya Mukhitova 22–23C; Nadya_Art 13BR; Irina Nowa 18TR; paper cut design 63BL; Paper Trident 61BL; Roi and Roi 55CL; Rumka vodki 17CL, 17BR, 30BL, 30CR, 31TL, 31CR; Salomi art 24R; Siberian Art 8CR, 39TR; Nadia Snopek 13BL; StockSmartStart 48BR; Stood Project 49BC; Storyet 35TR; Stranger Man 26BL; The img 38–39C; VectorShow 50C, 50BC, 51C; VikiVector 51TR; Marina Vishtak 44C; YUCALORA 52TR; YummyBuum 4TL, 9TL; Zhuma art 11BL, 21TR, 40BL; zuperia 35C.

FSC
www.fsc.org
MIX
Paper | Supporting responsible forestry
FSC® C104740

ISBN 978 1 80453 875 3
Printed in Dongguan, China
10 9 8 7 6 5 4 3 2 1

Welbeck Children's Books
An imprint of Hachette Children's Group
Part of Hodder & Stoughton Limited
Carmelite House, 50 Victoria Embankment
London EC4Y 0DZ

An Hachette UK Company
www.hachette.co.uk
www.hachettechildrens.co.uk

The authorised representative in the EEA is
Hachette Ireland, 8 Castlecourt Centre,
Dublin 15, D15 XTP3,
Ireland (email: info@hbgi.ie)

DREAMS

UNLOCK THE SECRETS OF YOUR DREAMS

Contents

Introduction 6
Common Dreams 8
Flying 10
Falling 12
Traveling 14
Being Lost 16
Water 18
The Science of Sleep 20
Numbers 22
Significant Numbers 24
Colors 26
Time 28
Seasons 30
Myths vs. Facts 32
Places 34
Rooms in Your House 36

School 38
The Body 40
Clothing 42
Types of Dreams 44
Animals 46
Birds 48
Bugs 50
Mythical Creatures 52
Ghosts 54
Dream Theorists 56
Disasters 58
Money 60
Food 62
Fame 64
Dreams and Media 66
Quiz 68
Glossary 70
Index 72

Introduction

Dreams. We all have them, but why? And most importantly, what do they mean? Inside this book, you will find the answers to these questions and more.

Your dreams are full of symbolism. They represent everything from experiences in your waking life to your innermost desires. The content of your dreams often reflects your feelings. For example, if you are stressed, you are more likely to have a nightmare about your teeth falling out, whereas if you are happy, you may dream about a pleasant experience such as flying.

There is an infinite number of things you can dream about, from hidden rooms to winning the lottery. On the following pages, we explore some of the most common dreams and what they represent. (Spoiler: they're not as random as you think!)

Learn what it means to dream about ghosts. The answer may surprise you!

You spend around **SIX YEARS** of your life dreaming and around 26 years of your life asleep.

Discover the difference between daydreams, lucid dreams, recurring dreams, and nightmares.

A brief history of dream interpretation

Dream interpretation dates back at least 4,000 years, with the oldest evidence of dream interpretation coming from the early civilizations of Mesopotamia and Egypt. Ancient Egyptians believed dreams could predict the future and recorded their interpretations on papyrus (a paperlike material made from a Nile plant), whereas ancient Greeks believed dreams were divine messages from gods. In ancient civilizations, professional dream interpreters existed, and even priests dabbled in the practice!

In the late 19th century, psychologists began taking an interest in dreams, with Sigmund Freud and Carl Jung leading the way. You can read about their theories on pages 56–57. The fascination with dreams and what they mean persists today, which is why you're reading this book!

Common Dreams

HOW MANY OF THESE COMMON DREAMS HAVE YOU HAD?

Some dreams are more common than others. From being naked to being chased, these dreams may feel wacky but are rooted in shared life experiences and reflect ordinary day-to-day emotions.

Strangely, common dreams are overwhelmingly negative! This could be because we are more likely to remember negative events than positive ones or because the brain focuses on what problems we need to solve.

FALLING
see pp12–13

BEING CHASED
see *Monsters* p52

TEETH FALLING OUT
see p41

UNABLE TO FIND A TOILET
see p36

AROUND THE WORLD

Common dreams vary slightly from country to country. This could be due to local surroundings, culture, and media influencing our dreams.

FLYING
see pp10–11

TAKING AN EXAM
see p38

BEING NAKED
see p42

BEING LATE
see p29

DYING
see p29

CRASHING A CAR
see p59

Flying

The ability to fly in dreams is often described as a thrilling experience. Flying with ease suggests you feel in charge, but if you're struggling to stay aloft, it could signify a sense of powerlessness. Flying dreams can also be symbolic of freedom, possibilities, and a strong reminder for you to never give up hope.

WITH WINGS

Flying with wings in a dream suggests you feel as free as a bird. Wings represent transcendence and spiritual growth, meaning change is in the air. The question is, are you ready to accept it?

THROUGH SPACE

To dream about flying through space represents a desire to escape the things that are holding you back. It is your subconscious telling you that you are ready for an out-of-this-world adventure, whether that be intergalactic or not!

WITHOUT WINGS

Dreaming about being a passenger in a plane suggests you feel powerless in your waking life and desire a fresh perspective. Flying a plane, however, symbolizes control and resilience: you are the pilot of your own destiny. Alternatively, dreaming about planes could just mean you need a vacation!

FLOATING

Levitating in dreams signifies contentment, represented as a feeling of weightlessness. You do not feel bogged down by earthly worries. However, if you are unable to stop floating, you may be feeling anxious or ungrounded in life.

IN A PLANE

To fly without wings in a dream indicates you feel in control of your life – you are able to achieve the impossible, and you have the confidence to do so. Embrace this quality, and you will soar to new heights.

Did you Know?

Dreams that feel especially real are known as vivid dreams. These types of dreams linger, and you can recall them in the morning.

Falling

Dreams about falling typically occur when you are anxious about something. These dreams can be thought of as the opposite of flying dreams, since they are often unpleasant and signify a lack of control. They can encourage you to take stock of what is overwhelming you so you can be more grounded in your waking life.

LOSING YOUR GRIP

Failing to hold onto something in a dream indicates a need for more support in your life. It is a sign that you feel overwhelmed and are metaphorically hanging on by a thread. Ask a loved one to help lift you up.

BEING PUSHED

Dreams about being pushed over have various interpretations. They may signify feeling "pushed around" by someone in your waking life. They could also represent a sense of powerlessness and being forced into a situation. Alternatively, this dream may act as a gentle nudge toward something that will eventually benefit you.

Did you Know?

The feeling of falling in a dream may be caused by hypnic jerks. These are involuntary muscle contractions that happen just as you fall asleep.

FROM A HEIGHT

Dreams about falling from a height are one of the most common dreams. They are believed to represent anxiety and a feeling of losing control in certain areas of your life. Falling dreams often end before you hit the ground, suggesting there is hope yet.

THROUGH THE FLOOR

To dream about falling through the floor indicates you feel unstable or insecure about something. A more positive reading, however, may imply you are on the brink of a transformation: the ground is shifting beneath you.

IN LOVE!

Dreaming about falling head over heels for someone, figuratively speaking, may reflect your true feelings toward a person. Though, if it's a stranger your dream self is in love with, it could mean you may be yearning for a connection or something new and exciting in your life!

Traveling

Traveling dreams may be a metaphor for the path you are taking in life. They can also be a sign that you are about to start a new journey. Dreams where you are an active traveler suggest you want adventure, whereas dreams set in in-between places, such as an airport or train station, indicate a time of change and reflection.

DRIVING A CAR

Dreams about driving a car can reflect your life's journey. If the drive is a successful one, it may mean you feel in control of your destiny. On the other hand, dreams about crashing a car suggest you feel out of control. It could be a warning that change is needed to get you back on course.

BY SHIP

Dreaming about traveling by ship suggests you are on a spiritual journey. This journey may be rocky and full of emotional ups and downs. It could also be your subconscious telling you to take risks and pursue new experiences. The world is your oyster!

BY TRAIN

Train dreams are associated with change and progress. They may symbolize that you are on track to achieve your goals and reach a desired destination. To dream about a train station—a place of transition—indicates you are going through a transformation.

VACATIONS

Dreams about going on vacation could mean you need a break. Perhaps you are bored and long for an adventure, or maybe you need an escape from life's pressures. Use this dream as motivation to get out of your slump. Why not create a vision board to inspire you?

AIRPORTS

Airports are liminal spaces—they sit between two places and represent change. Dreaming about being in an airport suggests you are on the cusp of a major life transition. You may feel in a state of flux right now, unsure about where you are heading. This dream could be a message that the path will reveal itself soon.

Did you Know?

Astral projection is the supposed act of leaving your body and traveling to distant places in your sleep. It is a kind of out-of-body experience that is viewed as a spiritual event.

Being Lost

To nobody's surprise, dreams about being lost can symbolize feeling lost in your waking life. Maybe you are lacking guidance or support, or maybe you just feel stuck. Pay attention to the landscapes of these dreams—they may be significant—and remember, sometimes you have to be lost to find yourself!

Did you Know?

Sleepwalkers can get seriously lost, though it is uncommon. One boy, Michael Dixon, ended up 100 miles away from home after a bizarre sleepwalking episode!

IN A CITY

To dream about being lost in a city suggests you feel overwhelmed in your waking life. Cities are loud, hectic places that may represent a troubled mind full of many thoughts competing for attention. This dream is a sign to take a breather: go outside and be in nature for a while.

GETTING SEPARATED

Dreams about getting separated from loved ones can represent many things, from separation anxiety to a breakdown in a relationship to a feeling of independence. How did you feel during the dream, and how do you feel reflecting on it? There may be a lot to learn from your answer.

AT SEA

If you find yourself lost at sea in a dream, you may be experiencing feelings of isolation. If this is true, don't be afraid to ask for support—everyone needs an anchor in their life. Alternatively, this dream may represent a lack of direction and a need for guidance. Politely ask your crew to step up!

IN A DESERT

Deserts are dangerous places without the right gear, and dreaming about being lost in one is a sign you feel helpless in your waking life. Consider what tools or support you may be lacking and come up with an action plan.

IN A FOREST

In dreams, being lost in a forest could signify fear and confusion, as forests can be scary places, full of mysterious sounds. Alternatively, it may symbolize a period of deep reflection, with the vast, unexplored landscape representing your expanding mind.

Water

Dreams about water represent the subconscious mind. If you find yourself struggling to stay afloat in a dream, it is likely you feel the same way in your waking life. To dream of turbulent waters symbolizes unrest, whereas to dream of calm waters indicates contentment. What you're doing in the water can also tell you how you are coping with these emotions.

Did you Know?

Sea otters often hold hands while they sleep so they don't drift apart. How adorable is that!?

SWIMMING

Dreams about swimming in calm, clear water represent a positive mindset and oneness with your surroundings. You are literally going with the flow! Dreaming about turbulent water, however, signifies inner turmoil: time to face what is bothering you.

WALKING ON WATER

Dreaming of walking on water indicates a heightened sense of self-belief. The possibilities may seem limitless to you right now! This dream can also represent faith and a connection to something greater than yourself.

DROWNING

Drowning in a dream is symbolic of suppressed emotions. It could be your subconscious telling you to let it all out so you don't sink under the pressure. Alternatively, this dream may be a warning against "drowning" in work or other responsibilities.

FLOODS

To dream of a raging flood suggests strong emotions are overwhelming you. Consider what might be causing you stress in your waking life. To see a gentle flood in your dream indicates a specific worry will soon be swept clean away.

RIVERS AND STREAMS

Unlike dreams about the ocean, which are varied and sometimes chaotic, dreams about rivers and streams typically represent contentment. You may be optimistic about the future, trusting that life is taking you in a positive direction.

The Science of Sleep

We spend one third of our life asleep but remember very little about what happens during that time. So what is sleep, and why do we do it?

Why do we sleep?

Your body operates on an internal 24-hour clock, called a circadian rhythm, which cycles between sleepiness and alertness. This is why you tend to feel sleepy at around the same time each night. Sometimes this rhythm gets disrupted when you stay up late, or if you travel to another time zone.

The exact purpose of sleep is still unknown, but we know that getting enough quality sleep is as crucial to our survival as food and water. Without it, your brain becomes foggy, and it gets really hard to concentrate and make decisions. Sleep affects almost every system in the body, from the brain, heart and lungs to the immune system. It's thought that during sleep your body is trying to repair itself. Scientists also think that sleep plays a major role in learning and memory, so make sure you get a good night's sleep before any tests!

Half Asleep

Whales and dolphins only allow one half of their brain to sleep at a time. This is so they can come up to the surface of the water to breathe and keep an eye out for danger.

Sleep stages

There are two basic types of sleep: rapid eye movement (REM) sleep and non-REM sleep. You cycle through all the stages of REM and non-REM sleep several times during the night. Each cycle lasts around 50 minutes in children and 90 minutes in adults.

NON-REM STAGE 1

This is the moment when you start to fall asleep and lasts for only a few minutes. Your breathing slows as your muscles relax and may occasionally twitch.

NON-REM STAGE 2

A period of light sleep where your heartbeat and breathing slow even more, your body temperature drops, and your eyes stop moving. Brain activity also starts to slow down. You spend more time in this stage than any other in the sleep cycle.

NON-REM STAGE 3

This is the deep sleep phase, when your heartbeat and breathing are at their slowest, and brain waves get even slower. It's hard to wake you up at this stage.

REM

Most dreaming occurs during this period of sleep. Brain activity increases, breathing becomes faster, and your eyes move rapidly from side to side under their lids. To stop you acting out your dreams, your arm and leg muscles become temporarily paralyzed.

How much sleep do we need?

Babies tend to sleep (on and off) up to 18 hours per day, schoolkids sleep around 8–11 hours, while adults make do with 7–9 hours, and elderly people often find they need even less. There is no magic number of sleep hours that works for everyone, which explains why your friend might bounce out of bed in the mornings while you would prefer to hit the snooze button. The most important thing is to get the amount of sleep that's right for you each night.

Numbers

Think dreaming about numbers is random? Numerology would disagree. According to this ancient study, numbers are full of meaning and have a special importance in people's lives. They can signify positive or negative change and maybe even point you in the right direction, if you choose to listen...

Dreaming of the number **ONE** symbolizes individuality, leadership, and interconnectedness with the universe.

2

The number **TWO** represents balance and harmony. To dream of it is a sign to reflect on your relationships.

3

The number **THREE** signifies the mind, body, and soul; seeing it in your dreams is a wake-up call to embrace your spiritual side.

4

FOUR is a no-nonsense number, representing, among other things, the four elements of earth, water, air, and fire. Dreaming of it suggests you crave stability and structure in life.

Did you Know?

It's thought the average person has 3–6 dreams per night, with each dream lasting between 5–20 minutes.

5

Dreaming about the number **FIVE** is a positive sign because it signifies great change is on the horizon.

6

In numerology, the number **SIX** is associated with caring. It tends to show up in dreams when you or someone else in your life needs emotional support.

7

It's called lucky number **SEVEN** for a reason. Dreaming about this number suggests success and good fortune are on the cards.

8

The number **EIGHT** represents achievement and abundance. Its appearance in your dreams is a sign you are on the right path to achieving your goals.

9

Dreaming about the number **NINE** is associated with completion and wisdom. Its appearance is a message of encouragement to help finish something.

Significant Numbers

As you have seen, all numbers are symbolic—but in dreams, the appearance of some are more significant than others. These unique numbers may represent cultural superstitions or dates personal to you. Use this guide as a starting point, but know that with these types of dreams, you are often the best interpreter.

ANGEL NUMBERS

Angel numbers are number sequences, such as 111 or 333, that are thought to have spiritual significance and convey a special message from the universe. Each sequence has its own meaning, and they can appear in dreams as an omen or guide.

UNLUCKY NUMBERS

Different cultures consider different numbers unlucky. For example, the number 13 is generally considered unlucky in the West, and dreaming about it is thought to represent bad luck. However, what is considered unlucky in one culture may be lucky in another—so keep that in mind the next time you dream about a "bad" number.

RECURRING NUMBERS

If you keep dreaming of a certain number or sequence of numbers, don't ignore it—there may be something to it. To find out what specific numbers in dreams mean, turn to pp 22–23.

Did you Know?

You forget most of your dreams. It's estimated people typically forget around 90% of their dreams upon waking up.

SPECIFIC DATES

Dreams about specific dates are said to foretell new events or experiences or encourage you to reflect on past events. The symbolism of special dates is highly personal. Only you can tell what these dates reflect—for example, a birthday or anniversary—and what they represent to you.

LOTTERY NUMBERS

Wouldn't it be great if you could foresee winning lottery numbers in your dreams? Unfortunately, we shouldn't take this sort of dream literally; it's unlikely they will make you a millionaire, but they could be a sign that you will soon run into good fortune.

Colors

Colors have great significance in dreams. They may manifest as moods or feelings and can be a strong reflection of our emotional state. Vibrant colors typically represent positive emotions, whereas dark colors tend to be associated with negative ones. However, colors in dreams are not always so black and white, as you will see.

BLACK

The color black is associated with fear, anxiety, and heaviness. In dreams, it can represent mystery or symbolic death. But fear not! The color black also serves as a metaphor for rebirth—for shedding the darkness and embracing the light.

RED

Red represents danger, but it also represents passion. If you are seeing a lot of red in your dreams, you are likely experiencing strong emotions toward something. Take it as a warning sign to address these feelings before they consume you.

YELLOW

Yellow is the color of warmth, joy, and creativity. If your dreams are bathed in yellow, like sunshine on a hot summer's day, you might be feeling optimistic about the future.

WHITE

Dreaming in white is thought to be a good omen. The color white represents purity, hope, and enlightenment and is commonly associated with new beginnings. Stay open to new experiences in your waking life.

BLUE

Don't feel blue if you dream in blue—it doesn't automatically mean you are experiencing depression. In fact, in color psychology, blue is seen as a calm and relaxing hue. If you dream of blue skies and vast oceans, your mind is likely at ease.

Did you Know?

According to studies, not everyone dreams in color. Some people report dreaming in black and white, some or even all of the time.

Time

Time dreams represent an awareness of time passing and are a reminder that it is never "too late" to change your life. Dreaming about the past indicates you may be holding onto something, whereas dreaming about the future allows you to explore possibilities and set goals. Dreams about the end of time signify that you are undergoing a transformation.

DEADLINES

Deadlines are inevitably stressful, and dreaming about them is a sign you are stressed beyond belief! Is there something you've been putting off? An assignment, perhaps? In which case, this may be your sign to stop procrastinating.

TIME TRAVEL

Time traveling in dreams represents a desire to escape reality. Traveling to the past in your dream suggests you have old wounds that need healing. Traveling to the future reflects an adventurous spirit—you are curious about what's in store and open to exploring new possibilities.

RUNNING LATE

To dream about running late indicates you feel overwhelmed and unprepared in your waking life. You may be finding it hard to meet your own expectations or the demands of others. Dreams of this kind are a reminder to slow down. Don't burn yourself out racing to the finish line!

END OF TIME

Dreams about the end of time—whether that be dreams about the apocalypse or death—aren't as doom and gloom as they may seem. Rather, they indicate the ending of one chapter and beginning of another. What will this new phase of your life look like?

Did you Know?

Tasks can take much longer to complete in dreams than in real life. Nobody really knows why, but one theory is that the slower processing of the brain during REM sleep may be to blame.

AGE

Age dreams generally represent curiosity or anxiety about the passage of time. Dreaming about being a baby or a young child may mean you feel vulnerable or have unresolved childhood issues that need addressing. Dreams about old age signify gaining wisdom and can be a mirror of your subconscious desires for the future.

Seasons

Dreaming of the seasons has many interpretations. Dreams set in spring and fall, which are known as transitional seasons, indicate change and stepping into a new you. Summer dreams are pleasant and jolly, representing a positive state of mind, whereas dreams about winter are more somber, encouraging you to reflect on your life.

SPRING

Dreaming of spring represents growth and new beginnings. You may have recently gone through a dark period in your life; this dream is a sign those days are over. It is time to break free from your cocoon and spread your wings.

SUMMER

Summer is associated with fun, relaxation, and, of course, vacations. Dreaming about summer signifies positive energy and emotional fulfillment. You likely feel content in life and optimistic about the future—maybe there's an exciting trip on the horizon?

WINTER

Dreams about winter represent a need for rest and reflection. It's time to hang up the metaphorical bathing suit and get cozy. Now might be a good time to lean into journaling and self-care. What revelations might you make about yourself in the quiet landscape of your mind?

FALL

Fall is a transitional season, and dreaming of it suggests you too are going through some life changes. Dreams of this sort are a message to let go of what is no longer serving you. Think about what you want to take into this new season of your life.

Did you Know?

When the seasons change, our sleep, and subsequently our dreams, are affected. Do you dream more or less during a particular season?

SEASONAL HOLIDAYS

Dreams about Christmas and other related holidays mean different things to different people. For some, Christmas symbolizes joy, nostalgia, and a feeling of togetherness. For others, it represents a period of stress and anxiety. How you feel about your Christmas dream indicates what you desire: companionship or alone time.

Dreaming Myths vs. Facts

People loooove to talk about their dreams and dreaming, so much so that it can be hard to differentiate between what is true and what is false. Do animals dream? Does cheese cause nightmares? Read on to find out...

Facts

1 Nobody knows why we do it!

There are many theories as to why we dream, but not one solid answer. One theory is that dreaming helps the brain process and store information and build memories.

2 Daydreaming has benefits.

Daydreaming is often thought of as a wasteful activity, but the benefits are clear. Research argues daydreaming improves creativity, helps the brain solve problems, and, most importantly, makes us feel good.

3 Cats and dogs dream too.

Yes—our furry friends really do dream. They have REM sleep just like us, and they too most likely dream about what they see in their waking life.

4 Children are more likely to have nightmares.

Anyone can suffer from nightmares, but they are more typical in children. This could be because children have more vivid imaginations and feel more vulnerable than adults.

5 Everybody dreams.

Not everyone can recall their dreams, but everybody dreams. In fact, people dream every night. Dreams can happen during any stage of sleep, but vivid dreams are most likely to occur during the REM stage.

A Strange Phenomenon

Sleep paralysis happens between the stages of wakefulness and sleep. In this state, you are conscious but unable to move, and you may experience hallucinations. It can be scary, but it is physically harmless.

Myths

1 You cannot control your dreams.

A lucid dream is a type of dream in which the dreamer is aware they are dreaming and can influence their dream – for example, changing the plot and characters. Lucid dreams are pretty rare, which makes them even cooler!

2 Eating cheese before bed gives you nightmares.

Despite the rumors, there is no solid proof that eating cheese before bed causes nightmares. Eating any food late at night is not a good idea, however, as it can negatively affect your sleep quality and health.

3 Sleepwalkers act out their dreams.

Sleepwalking occurs during non-REM sleep, whereas dreams typically happen during REM sleep. The idea that it's dangerous to wake a sleepwalker is also a myth, although it isn't very wise because you could scare them.

4 Dreams have no purpose.

Even those who believe dreams have no meaning can usually agree that they have a purpose. As we've established, what that purpose is depends on the scientist you ask!

5 If you dream it, it'll come true.

Sometimes, the things we dream about happen, but most of the time, they don't—and that's a good thing! We'd all like to win the lottery, but not many of us would like to be chased by zombies.

Places

The places you visit in dreams are a great indicator of how you feel about your life and surroundings. The atmosphere and landscape are the most important things. Is the place calm and comforting? Or is it scary and overwhelming? The answer is generally a reflection of how we feel about our real-world situation, so pay close attention.

FAMILIAR PLACES

Dreaming about being in a familiar place, such as your home, suggests a sense of comfort and security in your waking life. A place from your past may mean you are feeling nostalgic or want to reconnect with your roots.

MAGICAL PLACES

Visiting a magical place in a dream is, well, a dream! Magical places differ for everyone, so how does yours look? Is it colorful or muted, full of people or wildlife? Make a list—that kind of place might be your heart's calling!

HAUNTED HOUSES

Dreaming about a haunted house or other spooky setting means you've either been watching too many scary films or you're feeling fearful about life. Perhaps something from the past is haunting you, or you're afraid of what's around the corner... whatever the issue is, don't ghost it! Instead, face your demons head-on.

Did you Know?

Déjà vu, which is the feeling that you have already experienced something, can occur in dreams. This is likely because dreams are linked to memories.

HOSPITALS

Dreaming about being in a hospital can symbolize suffering and old wounds that need addressing. It may be a message to take better care of your health or wellbeing. Alternatively, this dream can indicate you have recently taken some necessary steps toward healing.

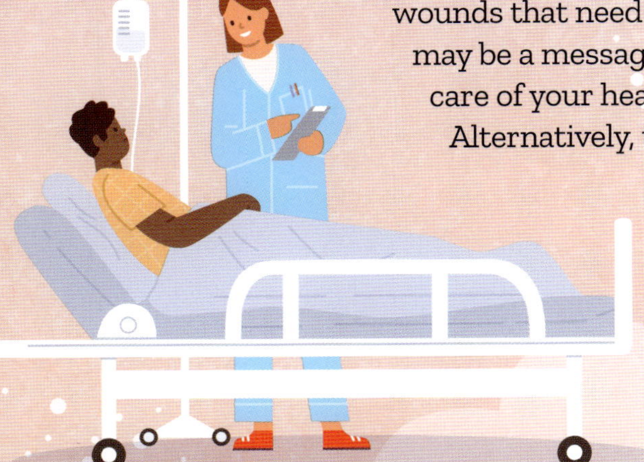

UNKNOWN PLACES

Visiting unknown places in a dream represents a longing to explore and might be a sign that you are about to embark on a new journey. Sometimes unknown places are actually familiar places but warped—these dreams hint at your potential for transformation.

Rooms in Your House

Dreaming about rooms in your house represents aspects of yourself that are known or undiscovered. They encourage you to reflect deeply on your identity and relationship with others by reminding you of your place in the world. Dreams about hidden rooms are perhaps the most exciting, signifying untapped potential.

BEDROOM

To dream of a bedroom symbolizes peace of mind and comfort since your bedroom is your sanctuary. It is also a place of privacy, meaning dreams set here may reflect your innermost thoughts and desires.

BATHROOM

Dreaming of a bathroom can represent a desire for catharsis—a wish to purge the negative emotions that are bothering you and start afresh. Being unable to find a toilet in a dream can signify helplessness, embarrassment, or pent-up feelings that need to be released.

LIVING ROOM

Dreaming of a living room may indicate a need for intimacy and connection, as the living room is the social hub of the house. Dreams of this sort may also be a sign to reflect on the way you present yourself to the world.

KITCHEN

Creations are made in the kitchen, and dreaming about one may be a metaphor for self-transformation. Dreams about cooking a meal may represent your inner creativity and desire to nurture others, such as your family and friends.

HIDDEN ROOMS

Dreams about hidden rooms are common and represent undiscovered parts of yourself. They are invitations to explore your own potential and develop your personality. What kind of things will you discover?

Did you Know?

It's common to struggle to sleep in a new place. It may be your body's way of keeping you safe in your new surroundings.

School

School dreams are usually a reflection of our perceived abilities: do you feel like you can do anything or nothing at all? If you find yourself sitting in class or taking a test in your dream, there's a strong likelihood you feel stressed in your waking life. Examine what is causing this—maybe it is school itself?

BEING IN SCHOOL

Dreams about being in school are common. They symbolize learning and can be accompanied by feelings of anxiety. Toss that anxiety aside and focus on the positives instead. What lessons have you learned recently?

TAKING AN EXAM

Dreams about exams are associated with stress. They indicate that you feel under pressure or scrutiny in your waking life. Dreaming about an exam you didn't study for suggests you feel underprepared about something. It might be a good idea to write a to-do list!

Did you Know?

The scientific study of dreams is known as oneirology. It is not the same as dream interpretation, which focuses on symbolism.

PUBLIC SPEAKING

Public speaking dreams may indicate social anxiety, but they could also represent a desire to be heard. This desire may be subconscious—you might be a shy person to whom the thought of public speaking sounds unbearable! However, this dream suggests it's not the attention you crave but the acknowledgement of your thoughts and opinions.

GRADUATING

Graduating in your dream represents a sense of achievement and personal growth. It is a sign that you should feel proud of yourself. Perhaps you have recently accomplished something difficult? In which case, take the time to celebrate yourself. You deserve it!

GRADES

Dreaming about good grades suggests you feel confident in your abilities, whereas dreaming about bad grades symbolizes low self-confidence. The takeaway from these dreams is to keep giving it your best shot and to work on your self-esteem if you fall into the second group.

The Body

Dreams relating to the body have less to do with appearance than you might think. More often, they are a reflection of our general concerns and fears. Feeling like you have a loose grip on your life can manifest as dreams about your teeth and hair falling out, but not all dreams about the body are scary; some are simply insightful.

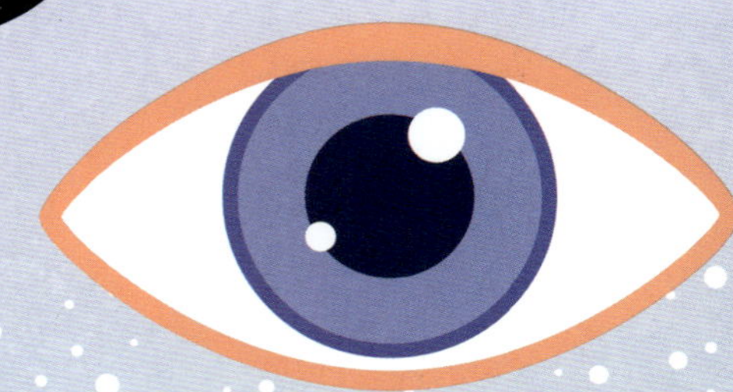

BONES

Bones are the foundation of us. To dream of unearthing bones represents uncovering something new about yourself or the need for change. Dreaming about broken bones suggests your foundation is shaky.

EYES

Eyes in dreams symbolize perspective, intuition, and awareness. Depending on whether your eyes are open or closed in your dream, it could be your mind's way of telling you to "open your eyes" to a certain situation or that you are becoming more aware of your surroundings.

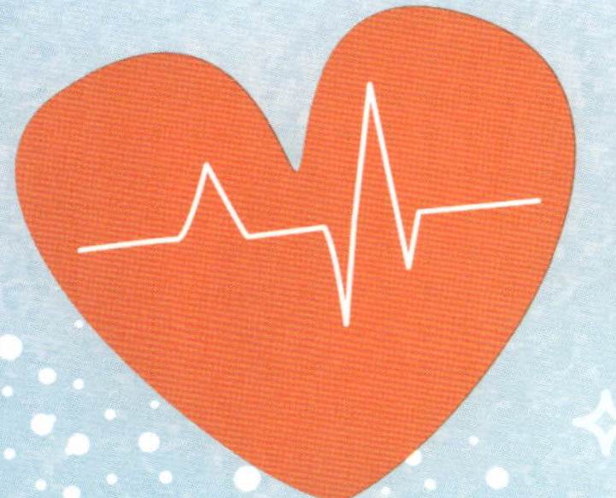

BLOOD

Dreams about blood can be scary, but their symbolic meaning isn't inherently negative. While on the one hand, blood represents pain and suffering, on the other, it represents energy and vitality. These dreams may be preparing you for challenges ahead—challenges you have the strength to overcome.

Did you Know?

During deep sleep, your body works to repair and restore itself. This is just one of the reasons why sleep is so important—especially when you are sick!

HAIR

Dreaming about getting a haircut indicates a desire to change something in your life, whether that be your appearance or something else. Dreams about hair loss are frightening and symbolize stress and vulnerability. Speak to somebody if this rings true to you.

TEETH

Almost everyone has dreamt about their teeth falling out. This common dream —or should we say nightmare!— is associated with feelings of anxiety and insecurity. Similarly, if you dream about your teeth breaking, this could mean you feel under extreme pressure.

Clothing

Clothes are a form of self-expression and can communicate many things, from our social status to our taste in music. Unsurprisingly then, dreams about clothes are centered around our sense of identity. The clothes you wear (or don't wear!) in a dream, and your attitude toward them, can say a lot about how you view yourself.

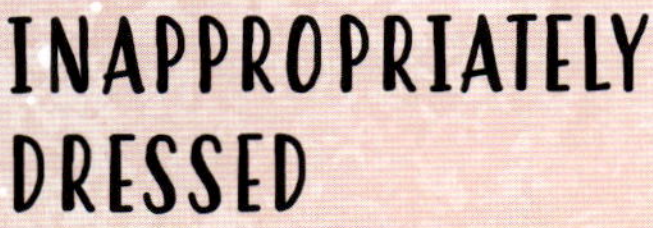

INAPPROPRIATELY DRESSED

Being inappropriately dressed in a dream, for example, wearing torn or dirty clothes or clothes that make you stand out, represents feelings of shame and embarrassment. It is a sign that you feel insecure about your social position and should learn to accept yourself.

NAKED IN PUBLIC

Dreaming about being naked in public indicates you feel vulnerable and are concerned about how others perceive you. Maybe you feel exposed, like everyone knows your secrets, or perhaps you suffer from low self-esteem. Focus on building confidence and these negative emotions should lessen.

Did you Know?

Pajamas date back to the Ottoman Empire of the 13th century. The word "pajama" comes from the Hindi "paejama," which translates to "leg covering."

CHANGING CLOTHES

Changing clothes in your dream represents transformation and "trying on" different identities. You may be stepping into a new role or chapter of your life soon. Think about the kind of changes you'd like to make: what aspects of yourself would you like to work on or keep the same?

BUYING CLOTHES

To dream about buying clothes suggests you want to fit in in your waking life. Alternatively, it may symbolize a desire for change. Consider which interpretation here suits you. If it is the first, you might want to ask yourself why you feel the need to blend in.

Types of Dreams

Dreams come in all shapes and sizes. You likely have an idea about daydreams and nightmares, but what about lucid dreams or night terrors? (No, they're not the same as nightmares.) Read on to find out about the main types of dreams and impress your friends with your newfound knowledge...

Daydreams

Daydreams are pleasant thoughts you have while you are awake. They can be incredibly absorbing and make you forget about the present. Common things to daydream about include the future and crushes!

2 Regular dreams

Regular dreams are the most common type of dreams that occur during REM sleep. They can feature familiar things, people, and places or seem illogical. You can assume that when we mention dreams in this book, we are referring to regular dreams.

3 Night terrors

As opposed to nightmares, which usually occur during REM sleep, night terrors typically happen during non-REM sleep, and you are unlikely to remember them when you wake up. During a night terror, you might scream or thrash about, though they are ultimately not harmful.

4 Nightmares

Nightmares are unpleasant dreams that cause a strong emotional response, such as fear or anxiety. You are likely to wake up from a nightmare and remember it clearly. Common nightmares include falling, losing your teeth, or getting injured.

5 Lucid dreams

A lucid dream is a dream where you are asleep but aware that you are dreaming. Lucid dreams can be very vivid and realistic. Some people who lucid dream can control their dreams, influencing the narrative.

6 False awakening dreams

Dreams about waking up when you're actually still dreaming are called false awakening dreams. They can be caused by insomnia, a sleep disorder that makes it hard to fall or stay asleep, or other sleep problems.

7 Recurring dreams

Recurring dreams are repeated dreams with a similar narrative. For example, you might dream about the same theme, location, or person night after night. The things that keep coming up in your dreams might be important to you in your waking life.

STAY TUNED

Some people experience progressive dreams. These dreams continue over multiple nights, picking up from where they left off the previous night —sort of like a TV show!

Animals

Dreams about animals are as varied as animals themselves! For example, dreams about dogs are thought to symbolize companionship and the relationships in your life, whereas dreams about lions are believed to reflect courage and strength. They are some of the easiest dreams to interpret since their symbolism is closely linked to the qualities of the animals that appear in them.

SNAKES

Snake dreams symbolize rebirth from a snake's ability to shed its skin. Seeing a snake in your dream suggests you are undergoing a significant transformation. Alternatively, dreaming of snakes can represent fear and a need to confront what is troubling you.

DOGS

Dogs are associated with loyalty and companionship, and dreaming about them suggests it's time to reflect on your relationships. An angry dog in a dream may represent conflict or hostility toward others, whereas a friendly dog may symbolize a close friend in your life.

LIONS

Lions symbolize courage and strength. To see a lion in your dream is a good sign that you have the ability to overcome any obstacles you may be facing. Lions also represent leadership, which suggests you have that quality within you. How will you use it?

CATS

Dreams about cats are thought to represent creativity, femininity, and independence. Some believe seeing a cat in your dream signifies misfortune. This probably comes from the myth that black cats are unlucky.

Did you Know?

Evidence suggests all mammals have the potential to dream. Wouldn't it be interesting to know what exactly they dream about?

BEARS

Dreaming about bears indicates you feel angry toward someone or something. However, if the bear is a friendly bear, it could be a sign that you feel protective of those around you: you have taken on the role of "mama bear."

Birds

Birds are powerful, majestic creatures, and dreaming about them is usually a good sign. In general, birds represent freedom and independence and could be a sign that you are close to achieving your goals. The type of bird you dream about can give you an insight into the state of your mind. For instance, doves are associated with peace, whereas owls represent wisdom.

DOVES

Dreaming of doves symbolizes peace and serenity. It suggests your mind and heart are open, meaning you are more able to forgive others and practice gratitude. This dream can also represent a loving relationship or a longing for a deep connection.

CROWS

Crows have a negative reputation as an omen of death. In dreams, however, they are more often welcomed as a symbol of rebirth and transformation. Seeing a crow in your dream is a sign you need to put the past to rest in order to meet the new you.

EAGLES

Eagles are high-flying birds that symbolize power, courage, and wisdom. Dreaming about an eagle suggests you are going through a spiritual awakening and have the insight and determination to achieve your goals, no matter life's obstacles.

OWLS

Owls are associated with wisdom and intuition. They have sharp senses and are thought to possess deep knowledge. Dreaming about them suggests you should learn to trust yourself more: your instincts are usually right.

PARROTS

Parrots appear in dreams to encourage you to think about how you communicate. Perhaps you could be a more active listener or express yourself better in conversations. Such dreams may also serve as a warning to avoid gossip—parrots aren't exactly the best secret-keepers!

Did you Know?

Birds can silently sing in their sleep. Researchers found that when a bird is asleep, its voice box can move in ways that are similar to when the bird is awake.

Bugs

Dreams about creepy crawlies often represent things in your life that are bothering you. Dreams about wasps and flies stand for irritating people in your life, while dreams about spiders are a sign you may feel stressed or overwhelmed. Dreams about butterflies are more positive, suggesting good change is on the horizon.

SPIDERS

Dreams about spiders generally symbolize stress and anxiety in your waking life. For example, dreaming about being bitten by a spider suggests you feel threatened or betrayed by someone close to you. On the other hand, spider dreams can represent creativity, from a spider's ability to weave intricate webs.

ANTS

Dreaming about ants can indicate you feel underappreciated for your work. For example, you might feel like you haven't been given enough credit in a group presentation. This dream could also be a sign to delegate tasks so you can avoid becoming overworked and overwhelmed.

WASPS

Wasp dreams represent feelings of annoyance and hostility. To dream about being stung by a wasp could mean someone close to you has caused you pain; similarly, dreaming about being swarmed by wasps indicates you feel defenseless. It might be time to stand up for yourself.

BUTTERFLIES

Dreaming of butterflies signifies new beginnings: the closing of one chapter and the start of another. This is because a butterfly undergoes a remarkable transformation during its life cycle. Who will *you* become?

Did you Know?

Insects appear in *Oneirocritica*, an ancient Greek book on dream interpretation written by Artemidorus Daldianus in the 2nd century A.D.

FLIES

Seeing a fly in your dream represents an annoying person in your life. Perhaps someone needs to buzz off! Dreaming of a room full of flies can mean that something that started out small is now getting out of control: time to stop ignoring it.

Mythical Creatures

From mermaids to monsters, dreams about mythical creatures are never dull. Sometimes scary, sometimes fun, their interpretations range from positive to negative to everything in between. Generally, though, these dreams represent fear, with the slaying of mythical creatures representing perceived power.

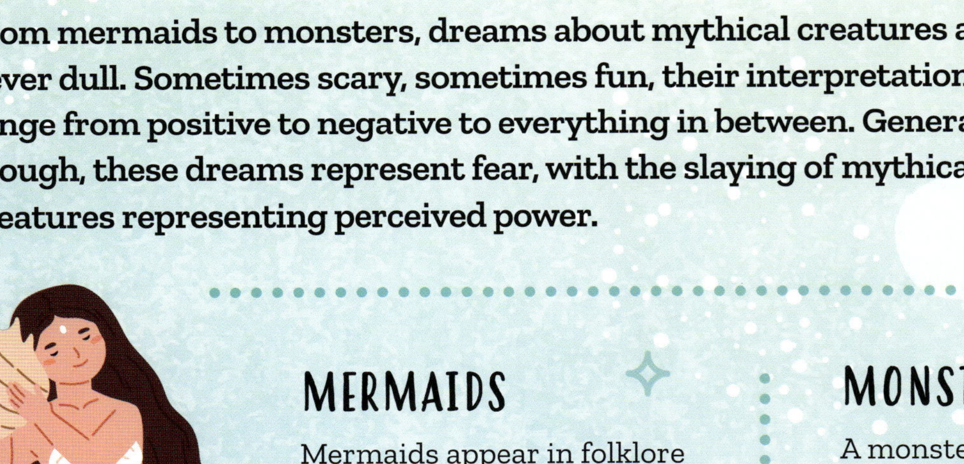

MERMAIDS

Mermaids appear in folklore as beautiful creatures with a dark side. They may appear to you in dreams as a warning about potential danger. Additionally, their association with the sea may symbolize a deep-seated desire for freedom.

MONSTERS

A monster in your dream is usually a metaphor for the things you are afraid of in your waking life. Slaying a monster in your dream suggests you will be successful in overcoming these fears, whereas to be chased or attacked by a monster indicates you should focus on managing your anxiety.

VAMPIRES

The appearance of this bloodsucking creature in your dream suggests there is somebody in your life who is sucking the energy out of you. Perhaps it is a friend who constantly takes from you but never gives back. Learn to protect yourself from these negative influences. You can leave the garlic at home.

Did you Know?

Watching horror films can cause nightmares—or, more accurately, the stress hormones produced by watching scary movies can cause nightmares!

DRAGONS

Although they may be frightening, dreaming about a dragon represents a strong will that can't be tamed. Harness this quality in your waking life, and you will be unstoppable! Just don't let your fiery nature get out of control...

ZOMBIES

In dreams, zombies represent helplessness—in particular, a feeling of being stuck. Depending on context, dreams of this sort may be telling you to fight back or surrender to the process. Think about the challenges you are facing right now and which course of action (or inaction) is best for you.

Ghosts

Dreams about ghosts are common. They can occur when you are grieving or if something is haunting you in your waking life. They may be a reminder of unfinished business to take care of. Ghosts in dreams are often scary, embodying fear and anxiety; sometimes, though, they look familiar. Perhaps a little too familiar...

SHADOWS

Shadow figures in dreams may represent hidden aspects of your identity. They can be an invitation to explore suppressed parts of your personality to better understand yourself. Sometimes, shadow dreams can be frightening, urging you to face lingering fears in your waking life.

EVIL SPIRITS

Dreams about evil spirits, such as demons, suggest you are surrounded by negative energy. Try to place the source of this negativity and distance yourself from it, if possible. If you dream about being possessed by an evil spirit, it might mean you feel controlled by someone: time to take back the reins!

FRIENDLY GHOULS

Occasionally, ghosts appear in dreams not to scare us but to represent unfinished business. A friendly ghost in your dream may be a metaphor for something in your past that you aren't ready to let go of. What's haunting you?

DEPARTED LOVED ONES

It isn't uncommon for loved ones who have passed away to appear in dreams. These dreams are a normal part of the grieving process and can provide comfort and reassurance. They may also bring a sense of closure.

YOURSELF AS A GHOST

Dreaming that you are a ghost can mean several things. Perhaps you feel invisible, or perhaps your subconscious is telling you not to waste your precious time on Earth and do all the things you want to do!

Did you Know?

Some believe dreams serve as gateways to the spiritual realm, allowing ancestors to communicate with the living.

Dream Theorists

There are many theories about dreams and just as many dream theorists, but two stand out above the rest. They are Sigmund Freud and Carl Jung, two influential psychologists.

SIGMUND FREUD

DREAMS AS WISH FULFILMENT

Sigmund Freud was the founder of psychoanalysis, a type of psychotherapy that aims to treat mental health issues by exploring a person's unconscious mind. He believed dreams represent a person's unconscious thoughts and desires and that they can be understood through the process of interpretation.

FAMOUS DREAM

Freud's own dreams inspired his dream theory. His dream, "Irma's Injection," in which a real-life patient of Freud's was ill, is one of the most famous dreams in the history of psychoanalysis!

CARL JUNG

DREAMS AS A WINDOW INTO THE UNCONSCIOUS MIND

Carl Jung founded the school of analytical psychology, which attempts to help individuals achieve an increased sense of self-knowledge and wholeness. He was inspired by Freud, but while Freud saw dreams as manifestations of repressed desires, Jung saw them as tools for personal growth and was interested in dream archetypes: symbols that have universal meanings across cultures.

Jung's MAIN ARCHETYPES

The self
The personality as a whole. It can appear as a hero or prophet in dreams.

The shadow
The hidden, repressed part of our identity. It can appear in dreams as a monster, snake, or other dark figure.

The persona
How we present ourselves to the world. It can take different forms in dreams.

The anima and animus
The anima represents the feminine part of a man's personality, whereas the animus represents the masculine part of a woman's personality. They can appear in dreams as female or male figures.

Disasters

Nobody likes disaster dreams, but everyone can learn something from them. These kinds of dreams usually occur when you're facing challenges in life, which can range from personal problems to issues in your relationships. They're here to say, enough is enough! No more bottling things up; it's time to express yourself.

WAR

War dreams may symbolize inner turmoil or conflict in relationships. They might also represent a desire for peace and harmony. If your defenses are up, ask why. If you want to see a change in the world, be that change.

NATURAL DISASTERS

Dreams about natural disasters can reflect unresolved issues. A dream about a flood signifies overwhelming emotions, whereas dreaming of a violent storm represents anger and frustration. Take the time to focus on your well-being, and remember, after the storm comes the calm!

APOCALYPSE

Dreams about an apocalypse could reflect real-world environmental concerns or emotional turmoil. Something in your waking life may be unsettling you, and you might feel unprepared to deal with it. Don't fret, and don't give up. These dreams don't represent the end—rather, they signify an awakening, aided by increased mental alertness.

Did you Know?

There are benefits to nightmares. You can learn a lot from them, and they can even prepare you to face real-life dangers!

ACCIDENTS

Plane crashes, car crashes, falling off buildings—the dreaming brain is very imaginative when it comes to ways of getting hurt. Don't panic! Just because you dreamt it, doesn't mean it will happen. These dreams are often driven by plain old fear and anxiety.

CRIME

Dreaming that you are a victim of crime suggests you feel vulnerable and powerless in your waking life. It is a sign to stand up for yourself and not let anybody take advantage of you.

Money

Money is associated with success, opportunities, and self-worth. As such, money dreams tend to revolve around these themes and can be a window into your state of mind. Positive dreams about money, such as winning or finding it, can symbolize optimism and good luck, whereas negative dreams about money may reflect a fear of being unsuccessful at something.

WINNING MONEY

Winning money in a dream indicates you feel joyful and optimistic about the direction you're heading in. You may feel like you're "winning" at life right now. Some also see this dream as a sign of good luck: either you are experiencing it, or you might run into it soon...

RECEIVING MONEY

Dreams about receiving money may represent one of two things. It could be a warning to control your spending habits, or it may represent the abundance of positive energy in your life. You might have achieved something impressive recently and are now reaping the rewards.

LOSING MONEY

Losing money in a dream may represent fear about finances, but it can also be a manifestation of other anxieties in your life. Perhaps you are afraid of losing something valuable to you or of being faced with a tough choice and making the wrong decision. Consider what can be gained from this insight.

Did you Know?

Dreams that appear to predict the future are common enough that they have a name: precognitive (premonition) dreams.

SPENDING MONEY

In general, dreams about spending money represent power, success, and authority. You might have run into wealth recently or feel rich in a metaphorical, contented way. To dream about spending money on other people indicates you are feeling generous.

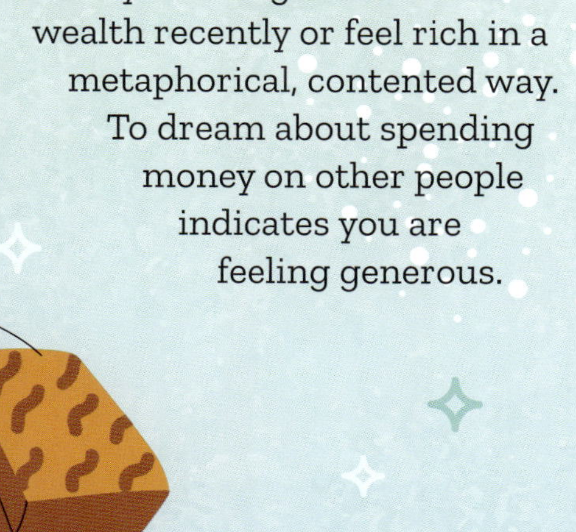

FINDING MONEY

Dreams about finding money suggest you are feeling adventurous and open to new experiences. They are uplifting dreams that can indicate good fortune awaits you. It's possible that having this dream means you have a positive attitude toward success: you believe you can achieve it, so you will get it.

Food

Food is nourishment, and it is essential to our survival. Dreams about an abundance of food can indicate you are emotionally fulfilled: your needs are met, and you do not long for anything. Dreams about dieting or being hungry, however, represent restriction and scarcity. Your subconscious may be bringing to your attention some kind of lack in your life.

Did you Know?

Spicy foods can increase body temperature, which can lead to increased brain activity during REM sleep and more vivid dreams.

COOKING

Dreams about cooking can symbolize nourishment in all forms, whether physical, spiritual, or emotional. They can also represent a love of creation and expressing yourself. Dreams of cooking in a social setting may indicate a desire to nurture others. Perhaps it's time to put on your chef's hat?

EATING

Eating food in your dreams may be a sign that you are satisfied and taking good care of yourself in your waking life. On the other hand, it could mean that you are after some sort of nourishment you are currently lacking.

FEASTS

A big feast in a dream is associated with abundance and celebration. It may represent a time of plenty or a period of socializing in your life. Eating too much in a dream, however, can signify you have bitten off more than you can chew, meaning you have taken on more tasks than you can handle.

HUNGER

Unsurprisingly, dreams about hunger can indicate a lack of fulfillment. You may literally be hungry or feel like you are being starved in some other area of your life. What are you longing for? And how can you feed your soul in the meantime?

DIETING

Dreams about dieting can symbolize a desire for control, just like dreams about breaking a diet are a sign you feel out of control. Dieting dreams could also mean that you are denying an important need. Maybe in your quest for control, you have neglected some emotional needs?

Fame

Fame is associated with success, admiration, and influence. If you dream about being famous or rubbing shoulders with the elite, it is likely you simply desire these things. Sometimes, though, fame dreams can point to feelings of insecurity. For example, dreams of infamy suggest you may be concerned about how others see you.

BEING FAMOUS

To dream about being famous suggests you yearn to be successful or popular. Depending on your own opinion of yourself, it might be a sign that these wishes will soon come to fruition or that you should have more confidence in yourself.

FAMOUS PEOPLE

Meeting or hanging out with a celebrity in your dream can indicate admiration or a need for guidance. You might look up to this person in your waking life. If so, what qualities do you like about them, and how can you put these qualities into practice?

Did you Know?

Dreams are a hot topic in the entertainment industry. There are hundreds of songs with the word "dream" in their title and countless films on the subject.

INFAMY

To dream about infamy—that is, being well-known for something bad—suggests you are anxious about how others perceive you. Guilt or shame over past actions may be eating you up. Reflect on these emotions and consider if they are helping or harming you.

ATTENDING A PRESTIGIOUS EVENT

Dreaming about attending a very formal event, such as a gala or award ceremony, indicates a need for validation or social recognition. It can symbolize a desire to be recognized for your talents, which may currently be overlooked.

BEING A LEADER

Dreams about being a leader can reflect confidence, ambition, and a desire to inspire others. You may want to be in a position of power where you can influence many, or want to make a difference on a more intimate scale. Whichever it is, this dream is encouragement to pursue your noble quest!

Dreams and Media

Now you know everything there is to know about dreams, it's time for some fun trivia. How many of these books, songs, and films do you know – and did you know they all came from dreams!?

THREE BOOKS INSPIRED BY DREAMS

1 *Frankenstein* by Mary Shelley

When Mary Shelley was 18 years old, she had a "waking dream" that inspired her to write *Frankenstein*. This book is credited with being the first true sci-fi novel.

2 *Stuart Little* by E.B. White

Asleep on a train, E.B. White dreamt of a courageous little boy with mouse-like features. Two decades later, *Stuart Little* was published and would become a childhood classic.

3 *Twilight* by Stephenie Meyer

The idea for *Twilight* came to Stephenie Meyer in the form of a "very vivid" dream about a human girl and a vampire who was in love with her. The resulting books are now among the best-selling series of all time.

THREE SONGS INSPIRED BY DREAMS

1 **"Yesterday"** **by The Beatles**

The melody for "Yesterday," the most covered song of all time, came to Paul McCartney in a dream. Upon waking, he hurried to the piano to play the tune before he forgot it.

2 **"All You Had to Do Was Stay"** **by Taylor Swift**

The lyrics for this song came from a dream Taylor Swift had about an ex, where all she could say was "stay" in a high-pitched voice (like in the song!).

3 **"Only If For A Night"** **by Florence + The Machine**

Florence Welch was inspired to write this song after an emotional dream she had about her late grandmother. The dream deeply moved the singer, who "woke up crying."

THREE FILMS / TV SHOWS INSPIRED BY DREAMS

1 ***Dreams*** **directed by Akira Kurosawa**

This Golden Globe-nominated film, which consists of eight short tales, is based on the director's own recurring dreams.

2 ***The Adventures of Sharkboy and Lavagirl*** **directed by Robert Rodriguez**

The script for this film was inspired by the dreams of the director's son.

3 ***Over the Garden Wall*** **created by Patrick McHale**

Series creator Patrick McHale said episode five of this animated miniseries was inspired by a dream he had about a house with apparently secret rooms.

DREAM ON!

Now you've seen what dreams can do, where will your dreams take you?

Okay, dream expert, let's see how much you've remembered. Choose the right answer to these multiple-choice questions, then see how well you did by checking the answers at the bottom...

How many dreams does the average person have per night?

a. 1–3
b. 3–6
c. 6–9

Which one of these statements is not true?

a. Cats and dogs dream.
b. Children are more likely to have nightmares.
c. Sleepwalkers act out their dreams.

3

What is the name for the scientific study of dreams?

a. Oneirology
b. Somnology
c. Psychology

What animals hold hands while sleeping?

a. Sea otters
b. Meerkats
c. Sloths

What are progressive dreams?

a. Dreams about waking up when you are still dreaming
b. Dreams you have while you are awake
c. Dreams that continue over multiple nights

Which one of these is not a common dream?

a. Falling
b. Joining the circus
c. Being chased

What is the name of Freud's famous dream?

a. Susan's Surgery
b. Enid's Exam
c. Irma's Injection

What is astral projection?

a. An out-of-body experience
b. Dreaming about the future
c. Very vivid dreams

Who dreamt the melody for "Yesterday"?

a. John Lennon
b. Paul McCartney
c. Taylor Swift

ANSWERS: **1.** b, **2.** c, **3.** a, **4.** a, **5.** c, **6.** b, **7.** c, **8.** a, **9.** b

GLOSSARY

Astral projection
An out-of-body experience that can be spontaneous or purposeful. It is believed that during astral projection, your spirit can travel to distant places.

Circadian rhythm
The changes your body goes through in a 24-hour cycle. Circadian rhythms tell your body when to eat, sleep, and wake.

Daydream
Pleasant thoughts while awake. They revolve around things that you would like to happen and can make you forget about the present.

Déjà vu
A feeling of having already experienced something before. Dreams can lead to this, by giving a sense of false familiarity.

Dream
A series of thoughts, images, or emotions that happen while you are asleep.

False awakening dream
A dream where you think you have woken up, but you are actually still asleep.

Fatigue
Extreme tiredness that can interfere with your ability to focus or carry out usual activities.

Hallucination
The experience of seeing, hearing, feeling, smelling, or tasting something that is not real. Hypnagogic hallucinations are hallucinations that happen as you fall asleep.

Hypnic jerk
A sudden, involuntary body movement that occurs in the transition between wakefulness and sleep.

Insomnia
A common sleep disorder that makes it difficult to fall or stay asleep. It can impair health and daytime functioning.

Interpretation
An explanation for something. For example, there can be multiple interpretations of one dream.

Lucid dream
A type of dream where you are aware you are dreaming and can sometimes control the dream.

Manifest
To show or reveal something clearly. In spirituality, it means using your thoughts to make something a reality.

Metaphor
A comparison between one thing and another, not to be taken literally.

Nightmare
An unpleasant dream that often causes you to wake up.

Night terror
Intense episodes of fear while asleep. During a night terror, you might scream or thrash about.

NREM sleep

Non-rapid eye movement sleep that occurs in stages 1–3 of sleep. In this phase, bodily functions slow down or stop altogether, and your body repairs itself.

Numerology

The study of the mystical significance of numbers.

Oneirology

The scientific study of dreams and their relationship to brain function.

Precognitive dream

A type of dream that appears to predict the future. Also known as a premonition dream.

Progressive dream

A series of dreams that occur over multiple nights and continue on from each other.

Psychoanalysis

A theory and field of research developed by Sigmund Freud that investigates the interaction between the conscious and unconscious mind.

Psychology

The scientific study of the human mind and how it might affect behavior.

Recurring dream

A specific dream that repeats itself over a long period of time. They can be positive or negative.

REM sleep

The stage of sleep where most dreams occur. It involves more brain activity than NREM sleep.

Sleep

A state of rest in which your eyes are closed and your consciousness is altered.

Sleep paralysis

A condition in which you are conscious but unable to move. It happens between the stages of wakefulness and sleep.

Sleepwalking

The act of walking around while you are asleep. Also known as somnambulism.

Spirituality

The belief in something greater than yourself. It is concerned with the spirit and soul rather than physical things.

Spiritual realm

According to spiritualism, a realm (area) inhabited by good and bad spirits.

Subconscious

The part of your mind that can influence your behavior although you are not aware of it.

Vision board

A collage of images and affirmations that represent your dreams and goals.

INDEX

A
accidents 59
age 29
airports 15
angel numbers 24
animals **46–47**
ants 50
apocalypse 59
astral projection 15

B
bathroom 36
bears 47
bedroom 36
birds **48–49**
black 26
blood 40
blue 27
body, the 20, **40–41**
bones 40
bugs **50–51**
butterflies 51

C
cats 32, 47
celebrities 64
circadian rhythm 20
clothing **42–43**
colors **26–27**
common dreams **8–9**
cooking 37, 62
crime 59
crows 48

D
Daldianus, Artemidorus 51
dates 25
daydreams 32, 44
deadlines 28
death 29
dieting 63
disasters **58–59**
dogs 32, 46
doves 48
dragons 53
dream theorists **56–57**
driving 14
drowning 19

E
eagles 49
eating 62
Egypt 7
Egyptians, ancient 7
evil spirits 54
eyes 40
exams 38

F
fall 31
falling **12–13**
 from a height 13
 in love 13
 through the floor 13
false awakening dreams 45
fame **64–65**
familiar places 34
feasts 63
flies 51
floating 11
floods 19
flying **10–11**
 in a plane 11
 through space 10
 with wings 10
 without wings 11
food **62–63**
Freud, Sigmund 7, 56

G
ghosts **54–55**
grades 39
graduating 39
Greeks, ancient 7

H
hair 41
haunted houses 35
hidden rooms 37
hospitals 35
hunger 63
hypnic jerks 13

I
infamy 65

J
Jung, Carl 7, 57

K
kitchen 37

L
late, running 29
leader 65
lions 47
living room 37
lost, being **16–17**
 in a city 16
 in a desert 17
 in a forest 17
 at sea 17
lottery 25
lucid dreams 33, 45

M
magical places 34
mermaids 52
Mesopotamia 7
money **60–61**
monsters 52
mythical creatures **52–53**
myths 33

N
natural disasters 58
night terrors 45
nightmares 45, 53, 59
non-REM sleep 21
nudity 42
numbers **22–23**
numerology 22

O
Oneirocritica 51
Ottoman Empire 43
owls 49

P
parrots 49
places **34–35**
precognitive dreams 61
progressive dreams 45
public speaking 39

R
recurring dreams 45
recurring numbers 25
red 26
REM sleep 21
rooms in your house **36–37**

S
school **38–39**
science of sleep, the **20–21**
seasonal holidays 31
seasons **30–31**
separation 16
shadows 54
significant numbers **24–25**
sleep paralysis 33
sleepwalking 16, 33
snakes 46
spiders 50
spiritual realm 55
spring 30
summer 30
swimming 18

T
teeth 41
time **28–29**
time travel 28
traveling **14–15**
 by ship 14
 by train 15

U
unknown places 35
unlucky numbers 24

V
vacations 15
vampires 53
vivid dreams 11

W
war 58
wasps 51
water **18–19**
white 27
winter 31

Y
yellow 27

Z
zombies 53